PRIMA LATI

An Introduction to Christian Latin

Second Edition

STUDENT BOOK

By Leigh Lowe

CLASSICAL TRIVIUM CORE SERIES

> **Your Next Latin Program**
> *Latina Christiana I*
> by Cheryl Lowe

Once you complete *Prima Latina*, the next recommended course is *Latina Christiana I*.

Latina Christiana flashcards may be used with Prima Latina

Prima Latina: Student Book
By Leigh Lowe

Published by:

Memoria Press
www.MemoriaPress.com

Second Edition 2003
First Edition 2002
ISBN # 1-930953-51-8

Prima Latina
2ND EDITION

PRONUNCIATION RULES

The Alphabet

The Latin alphabet has no "w". Words with "y" are of Greek origin.

Vowels

In Christian Latin vowels are usually long.

Vowel	Long	Example
a	'father' (ah)	ambulo
e	'they' (ay)	deus
i	'machine' (ee)	via
o	'no' (oh)	toga
u	'rule' (oo)	luna

Sometimes the vowels **e** and **i** tend toward the short vowel sounds ('Ed','it') as in 'mensa' and 'et'.

Diphthongs and digraphs

Digraph	Pronunciation	Example
ae	like *e* in 'they' (ay)	caelum
oe	like *e* in 'they' (ay)	proelium

Diphthong		
au	like ou in cow (ow)	laudo, nauta

Consonants

Most of the consonants are pronounced as in English, with the following exceptions.

Consonant	Pronunciation	Examples
c	soft before *e, i, ae, oe,* like *ch* in 'charity'	decem, caelum
c	hard before other letters, like *c* as in 'cut'	clamo, corona
g	soft before *e, i, ae, oe* like *g* as in 'germ'	regina, gemini
g	hard before other letters like *g* as in 'go'	toga, navigo
gn	like *gn* as in 'lasagne'	pugno
j	like *y* as in 'yet'	Jesus, judico
s	like *s* as in 'sing' (never like *z*)	tres, mensa
sc	like sh	discipulus
t	like *tsee*, when followed by *i* and a vowel	etiam

Prima Latina
Lessons

Practical Latin

Salve!   – Hello! (to one person)

Salvete!   – Hello! (to more than one person)

Lesson – The Alphabet

The building blocks of any language are the letters used to make words.

The English Alphabet

There are *26 letters* in the English alphabet.

The **alphabet** is made up of two types of letters:

      vowels   and   **consonants**.

A,E,I,O,U	**BCD FGH JKLMN PQRST VWXYZ** (all letters that are not vowels)

The Latin Alphabet

The Latin alphabet looks like the English alphabet EXCEPT:

There are only *25 letters* in the Latin **alphabet.**

The Latin alphabet has no **W**!

Latin has the same vowels as English, **A,E,I,O,U,** but they sound a little different. Here are the Latin Vowel sounds.

Vowel	*Latin Sound*
A	ah, as in father
E	ay, as in way
I	ee, as in see
O	oh, as in no
U	oo, as in boo

** Remember

Latin **E** sounds like an English long **A**.

Latin **I** sounds like an English long **E**.

Vocabulary

Practice saying the Latin **vowels** in each word.

1. ambulo	I walk
2. via	road
3. Deus	God
4. toga	toga
5. luna	moon

Latin Prayers

Oremus   **Let us pray**
Say this before each prayer.

Derivatives

ambulance   --a vehicle to carry those who cannot walk to the hospital (n.)
viaduct   --a roadway or bridge on piers (n.)
deity   --a god (n.)
lunar   --having to do with the moon (adj.)

Review Questions

1. How many letters are in the English alphabet? _____

2. How many letters are in the Latin alphabet? _____

3. What letter is missing from the Latin alphabet? _____

4. What are the two kinds of letters in the English alphabet? _____

_____

Translation

1. toga _____

2. Deus _____

3. ambulo _____

4. luna _____

5. via _____

Speaking Latin —Listen to the Lesson 1 track on your Prima Latina CD—

☐ Practice saying the Latin vowel sounds in order…ah, ay, ee, oh, oo.
Can you say them five times in a row?
How fast can you correctly say them?

☐ Practice saying, "Salve" or "Salvete" to your parents, brothers and sisters, or friends this week.

☐ Begin the prayer before each meal with "Oremus."

☐ Say each vocabulary word and its meaning five times.

Write and Learn

1. Write out the English alphabet.

    Circle the vowels and underline the consonants.

    _____

    _____

2. Write out the Latin alphabet for practice. Make sure to leave out or cross out the **W**!

    _____

    _____

3. Write each vocabulary word and its meaning twice.

    1. _____   _____

       _____   _____

    2. _____   _____

       _____   _____

    3. _____   _____

       _____   _____

    4. _____   _____

       _____   _____

    5. _____   _____

       _____   _____

Fun Practice: Draw a line to match the letter with its Latin sound.

A	ah
I	ee
U	ay
E	oh
O	oo

Practical Latin

Magister – Teacher (male)   Magistra – Teacher (female)

Lesson – Consonants and Diphthongs

Consonant Sounds:

Consonants	Latin Sound
c (before e, i, ae, & oe is soft)	ch, as in charity
c (before all other letters is hard)	k, as in cat
g (before e, i, ae, & oe is soft)	g, as in germ
g (before all other letters is hard)	g, as in good
j	y, as in yes
s	s, as in soap

Compare the soft and hard sounds of *c* and *g* in Latin & English:
- The soft *c* in Latin sounds like "ch" as in charity.
- The soft *c* in English sounds like "s" as in ceiling.
- The hard *c* is the same in Latin and English.
- The soft and hard *g* are the same in Latin and English.

Diphthongs:

In Latin, sometimes two letters have only one sound.
These letter pairs are called **diphthongs.**

Diphthongs	Latin Sound
ae	ay, as in way (English long A)
oe	ay, as in way (English long A)
au	ow, as in loud

Vocabulary

Practice saying the **consonant** sounds and **diphthongs**.

1. gloria   glory

2. Jesus   Jesus

3. laudo   I praise

4. clamo   I shout

5. caelum   heaven

Latin Prayers (The Sanctus)

* Each week, learn the bold portion of the prayer and add it to what you know.

Sanctus, Sanctus, Sanctus
Dominus Deus Sabbaoth.
Pleni sunt caeli et terra gloria Tua.
Hosanna in excelsis.
Benedictus qui venit in nomine Domini.
Hosanna in excelsis.

Holy, Holy, Holy
Lord God of Hosts.
Heaven and earth are full of Your glory.
Hosanna in the highest.
Blessed is he who comes in the name of the Lord.
Hosanna in the highest.

Derivatives

glorious   -- wonderful (adj.)

glorify   -- to exalt, worship or honor (v.)

Jesuit   -- a Roman Catholic order for men, called
           the Society of Jesus (n.)

laud   -- to praise (v.)

proclamation   -- an official announcement (n.)

celestial   -- heavenly (adj.)

Review Questions ════════════════════════════

    1. How many letters are in the English alphabet?_____

    2. What are the letters **A,E,I,O,U** called? _____

    3. What does a Latin **E** sound like? _____

    4. What does a Latin **I** sound like? _____

    5. What does a Latin **O** sound like? _____

Lesson 2 Questions ════════════════════════════

    1. How many letters are in the Latin alphabet? _____

    2. What consonant is missing in the Latin alphabet? _____

    3. What do you call two vowels that make one sound? _____

    4. What does a **J** sound like in Latin?_____

    5. List three diphthong pairs. _____

Translation ════════════════════════════

    1. caelum   _____

    2. gloria   _____

    3. Jesus   _____

    4. laudo   _____

    5. clamo   _____

Speaking Latin --Listen to the Lesson 2 track on your Prima Latina CD-- ════════

    ☐ Think of an English word that uses the following Latin consonant sounds:

        hard g, as in gloria   _____

        soft g, as surgite   _____

        soft c, as in caelum   _____

        hard c, as in clamo   _____

☐ Say each vocabulary word and its meaning five times.

☐ Address your teacher as "Magister" or "Magistra" from now on.

☐ Practice saying the Latin Prayers from Lessons 1 and 2, the Sanctus, five times.

Write and Learn

1. Write the six Latin consonants in the lesson and the Latin sounds that go with them.

_____   _____

_____   _____

_____   _____

_____   _____

_____   _____

_____   _____

_____

2. Write the three diphthongs in the lesson and the Latin sounds that go with them.

_____   _____   _____

3. Write each vocabulary word and its meaning twice.

1. _____   _____

_____   _____

2. _____   _____

_____   _____

3. _____   _____

_____   _____

4. _____   _____

_____   _____

5. _____   _____

_____   _____

Fun Practice

Think of a poem or song to help you remember the vowel sounds.

Practical Latin

Surge – Stand up
(one person)

Surgite – Stand up
(more than one person)

*Remember g before e and i is soft like *g* as in *germ*

Lesson – Verbs

Now that you have mastered letters and sounds, you can start making words! In any language, one of the most important kinds of words is a verb!
Without verbs we wouldn't get anything done!

Verbs are *ACTION* words. In many cases you can see the action.
Examples of action words:

run   jump   kick   sing

An easy way to tell if a word is a **verb** is write or say it in the blank below.

Verb-Finder Sentence: Can I _____?

If the sentence makes sense, you probably have filled in the blank with a **verb.**

Examples:

Can I run?   ✓ YES, so **run** is a **verb**.

Can I jump?   ✓ YES, so **jump** is a **verb**.

Can I kick?   ✓ YES, so **kick** is a **verb**.

Can I table?   ☒ NO, I cannot table.
This doesn't make sense, so **table** is not a **verb**.

Vocabulary

Notice the o at the end of the Latin verbs below:

1. navigo	I sail
2. porto	I carry
3. oro	I pray
4. laboro	I work
5. specto	I look at

Latin Prayers (The Sanctus)

Sanctus, Sanctus, Sanctus
Dominus Deus Sabbaoth.
Pleni sunt caeli et terra gloria Tua.
Hosanna in excelsis.
Benedictus qui venit in nomine Domini.
Hosanna in excelsis.

Holy, Holy, Holy
Lord God of Hosts.
Heaven and earth are full of Your glory.
Hosanna in the highest.
Blessed is he who comes in the name of the Lord.
Hosanna in the highest.

Derivatives

navigate -- to steer a ship or plane (v.)

navy -- a nation's ships OR a dark blue color (n.)

portable -- something that can be carried (adj.)

airport -- a place where aircraft land and take off (n.)

oral -- spoken, or having to do with the mouth (adj.)

oratory -- the art of public speaking (n.)

laboratory -- a place for scientific work or research (n.)

labor -- work, physical or mental exertion (n.)

spectacle -- a remarkable sight (n.)

spectacular -- remarkable, unusual (adj.)

Review Questions

1. List all the vowels in the English alphabet. _____, _____, _____, _____, _____

2. List the 3 diphthongs you learned about in Lesson 2. _____, _____, _____

3. How many vowels make up one diphthong? _____

4. What does a **J** sound like in Latin? _____

5. How do you say, "Hello, teacher" (female) in Latin? _____

Lesson 3 Questions

1. What are action words called? _____

2. What is the helpful Verb-Finder sentence? _____

3. What do you notice about all the words in the vocabulary list? Hint: They are all

   verbs so they all end in the letter _____ .

4. How do you say, "Stand up" to one person in Latin? _____

Translation

1. oro   _____

2. laboro   _____

3. porto   _____

4. specto   _____

5. navigo   _____

Speaking Latin --Listen to the Lesson 3 track on your Prima Latina CD--

☐ Say each vocabulary word and its meaning five times. Practice using the vowel and

   consonant sounds you learned in Lessons 1 and 2.

   (**Specto** has a short **e** sound, like "eh".)

☐ Every time you stand up today, practice saying, "Surge."

☐ Practice saying the Latin Prayer from Lessons 1, 2, 3, the Sanctus, five times.

Write and Learn

1. Write each vocabulary word and its meaning twice.

   1. _____   _____

      _____   _____

   2. _____   _____

      _____   _____

   3. _____   _____

      _____   _____

   4. _____   _____

      _____   _____

   5. _____   _____

      _____   _____

2. Think up 5 English verbs that are not in Lesson 3. Write them in the Verb-Finder Sentence below to make sure they are verbs. A sample has been done for you.

   Verb Finder Sentence   **Yes?**

   Can I _____ Jump _____ ?   ✓

   1. Can I _____?   ☐

   2. Can I _____?   ☐

   3. Can I _____?   ☐

   4. Can I _____?   ☐

   5. Can I _____?   ☐

Fun Practice   Circle the English verbs.

walk	tree	snap	climb
desk	book	shout	shoe
wish	sit	car	look
water	sail	beach	laugh

Practical Latin

Vale – Goodbye
(to one person)

Valete – Goodbye
(to more than one person)

Lesson – Invisible Verbs

Some verbs are **invisible verbs**.

You cannot always *see* them in *ACTION*, but they are verbs nonetheless.

Invisible action words are still verbs, they are just less obvious.

Examples of some **invisible verbs**:

think   hope   pray   love

Practice putting these **verbs** in our helpful **Verb-Finder sentence.**

> **Verb-Finder Sentence:** Can I _____?

Can I think?   ✓ YES! So **think** is a **verb**.

Can I hope?   ✓ YES! So **hope** is a **verb**.

Can I love?   ✓ YES! So **love** is a **verb**.

These words make sense in our Verb-Finder Sentence so they are verbs. Even though you can't always *see* someone think, hope, or love, it is something they can do.

Vocabulary

Notice the o at the end of the Latin verbs below.

1. amo	I love
2. adoro	I adore
3. habito	I live in
4. judico	I judge
5. paro	I prepare

Latin Prayers (The Sanctus)

Sanctus, Sanctus, Sanctus
Dominus Deus Sabbaoth.
Pleni sunt caeli et terra gloria Tua.
Hosanna in excelsis.
Benedictus qui venit in nomine Domini.
Hosanna in excelsis.

Holy, Holy, Holy
Lord God of Hosts.
Heaven and earth are full of Your glory.
Hosanna in the highest.
Blessed is he who comes in the name of the Lord.
Hosanna in the highest.

Derivatives

amorous	-- full of love (adj.)
adoration	-- great love or devotion (n.)
adorable	-- lovable (adj.)
habitat	-- a place where something or someone lives (n.)
judicial	-- having to do with judges, courts, and laws (adj.)
judgment	-- a decision or opinion (n.)
parachute	-- a device used to slow the speed of someone jumping from an airplane (n.)
preparation	-- getting ready, or making something in advance (n.)

Review Questions

1. What are action words called? _____

2. What do you call two vowels that make one sound? _____

3. What letter is missing from the Latin alphabet? _____

4. What word means, "Let us pray" in Latin? _____

5. What does a Latin **E** sound like? _____

Lesson 4 Questions

1. How can you tell if a word that does not show action is a verb (an invisible verb)?

   _____

2. What do you notice about all the Latin vocabulary words in Lesson 4?

   (Hint: look at the endings again.) _____

   _____

3. How do you say, "Goodbye" to one person in Latin? _____

4. How do you say, "Goodbye" to your entire family in Latin? _____

5. What do you call verbs you can't see in action? _____

Translate

1. habito   _____

2. amo   _____

3. paro   _____

4. judico   _____

5. adoro   _____

Speaking Latin --Listen to the Lesson 4 track on your Prima Latina CD--

☐ Say each vocabulary word and its meaning five times.

☐ Practice the vowel and consonant sounds you learned in Lessons 1 and 2. Say each five times.

☐ Say, "Goodbye" to your family in Latin this week.

☐ Practice Saying the Latin Prayers from Lessons 1 through 4, the Sanctus, five times.

Write and Learn

1. Write each vocabulary word and its meaning twice.

    1. _____   _____
       _____   _____

    2. _____   _____
       _____   _____

    3. _____   _____
       _____   _____

    4. _____   _____
       _____   _____

    5. _____   _____
       _____   _____

2. Think of eight invisible verbs in English. Write them on the lines below.
   Use the Verb-Finder sentence to make sure you are listing verbs.

   _____ _____ _____ _____

   _____ _____ _____ _____

Fun Practice

Get your favorite storybook. Find 6 invisible verbs while you read.

_____   _____   _____

_____   _____   _____

Practical Latin

Discipulus – student   Discipuli   – students
(sc has a 'sh' sound)

Lesson – Latin Verbs

ENGLISH VERBS

In English, verbs can start with any letter, end with any letter, and be as long or short as any other word.

English verbs look the same as any other English word.
Because you can't tell an English verb by looking at it, we have to use our Special Verb-Finder Sentence

LATIN VERBS

In Latin, **verbs** in their dictionary form look similar.

In a vocabulary list, Latin verbs all end in the letter "o"!

So, in English, we have to decide if a word is a verb by **thinking** about it.
But, in this book, we can usually decide if a Latin word is a verb by simply **looking** at it.

Vocabulary

Notice the **o** at the end of the Latin verbs below.

1. liber**o**		I free
2. narr**o**		I tell
3. pugn**o**		I fight
4. super**o**		I conquer
5. voc**o**		I call

Latin Prayers (The Sanctus)

Sanctus, Sanctus, Sanctus
Dominus Deus Sabbaoth.
Pleni sunt caeli et terra gloria Tua.
Hosanna in excelsis.

Holy, Holy, Holy
Lord God of Hosts.
Heaven and earth are full of Your glory.
Hosanna in the highest.

Benedictus qui venit in nomine Domini.

Hosanna in excelsis.

Blessed is he who comes in the name of the Lord.
Hosanna in the highest.

Derivatives

liberty	-- freedom (n.)
narrate	-- to tell about a story or event (v.)
narrator	-- the person telling about the story or event (n.)
pugnacious	-- in a fighting spirit (adj.)
superior	-- excellent (adj.)
vocal	-- something to do with speaking or singing (adj.)
vocabulary	-- a list of words (n.)

Review Questions

1. How would you describe a verb? _____

2. Name two types of letters in the alphabet. _____

3. List three Latin action verbs you have learned so far. _____

   _____

4. List three Latin invisible verbs you have learned so far. _____

   _____

5. How do you say, "Goodbye, Teacher" (male) in Latin? _____

Lesson 5 Questions

1. In what letter do all simple Latin verbs end? _____

2. Is the letter at the end of all English verbs the same? _____

3. What is the Latin word for *one* student? _____

4. What is the Latin word for *many* students? _____

Translate

1. voco   _____

2. supero   _____

3. narro   _____

4. pugno   _____

5. libero   _____

Speaking Latin   --Listen to the Lesson 5 track on your Prima Latina CD--

☐ Say each vocabulary word and its meaning five times. Practice the vowel and consonant sounds you learned in Lessons 1 and 2.

☐ Practice saying the Latin Prayers from Lessons 1 through 5, the Sanctus, five times.

Write and Learn

1. Write each vocabulary word and its meaning twice.

1. _____   _____

   _____   _____

2. _____   _____

   _____   _____

3. _____   _____

   _____   _____

4. _____   _____

   _____   _____

5. _____   _____

   _____   _____

2. Think of eight verbs you performed today. Write them below, in the order you completed them. Put an **A** by the action verbs and an **I** by the invisible verbs.

_____   _____

_____   _____

_____   _____

_____   _____

Fun Practice

Circle the Latin verbs.

terra	voco	paro	Roma
porto	herba	aqua	laboro
via	specto	navigo	memoria
Italia	laudo	lingua	voco

Vocabulary

Verbs

laudo	I praise
clamo	I shout
ambulo	I walk
navigo	I sail
porto	I carry
oro	I pray
laboro	I work
specto	I look at
amo	I love
adoro	I adore
habito	I live in
judico	I judge
paro	I prepare
libero	I free
narro	I tell
pugno	I fight
supero	I conquer
voco	I call

Nouns

via	road
Deus	God
toga	toga
luna	moon
gloria	glory
Jesus	Jesus
caelum	heaven

> **Latin Song**-- on *Lingua Angelica CD*
> "Dona Nobis Pacem"
> -Grant us Peace

Practical Latin

salve	hello (to one person)
salvete	hello (to more than one person)
magister	teacher (male)
magistra	teacher (female)
surge	stand up (to one person)
surgite	stand up (to more than one person)
vale	goodbye (to one person)
valete	goodbye (to more than one person)
discipulus	student
discipuli	students

Latin Prayers – The Sanctus

Sanctus, Sanctus, Sanctus	Holy, Holy, Holy
Dominus Deus Sabbaoth.	Lord God of Hosts.
Pleni sunt caeli et terra gloria Tua.	Heaven and earth are full of Your glory.
Hosanna in excelsis.	Hosanna in the highest.
Benedictus qui venit in nomine Domini.	Blessed is he who comes in the name of the Lord.
Hosanna in excelsis.	Hosanna in the highest.

A. Copy all vocabulary words and translate.

Extra: Write one derivative next to each word.

	Word	Translation	Derivative
1.	_____	_____	_____
2.	_____	_____	_____
3.	_____	_____	_____
4.	_____	_____	_____
5.	_____	_____	_____
6.	_____	_____	_____
7.	_____	_____	_____
8.	_____	_____	_____
9.	_____	_____	_____
10.	_____	_____	_____
11.	_____	_____	_____
12.	_____	_____	_____
13.	_____	_____	_____
14.	_____	_____	_____
15.	_____	_____	_____
16.	_____	_____	_____
17.	_____	_____	_____
18.	_____	_____	_____
19.	_____	_____	_____
20.	_____	_____	_____
21.	_____	_____	_____
22.	_____	_____	_____
23.	_____	_____	_____
24.	_____	_____	_____
25.	_____	_____	_____

B. Answer the following questions in English.

1. How many letters are in the Latin alphabet? _____

2. What letter is missing from the Latin alphabet? _____

3. How many vowels are there? _____

4. What does a **J** sound like in Latin? _____

5. What does an **E** sound like in Latin? _____

6. What does an **I** sound like in Latin? _____

7. What are the two kinds of letters? _____

8. What are words that show action called? _____

9. In what letter do all simple Latin verbs end? _____

10. What sentence helps you determine if a word is a verb? _____

C. Practice saying the Sanctus completely.
Say it five times from memory. Write it once in Latin for practice.

_____

_____

_____

_____

_____

_____

D. Answer the following questions in Latin.

1. What do you say when you first see someone? _____

2. What would you call your female teacher? _____

   What would you call your male teacher? _____

3. What does your teacher tell the class before the Pledge of Allegiance? _____

4. What do you say when you are leaving your entire family? _____

   What do you say when you are leaving a friend? _____

5. What do you call yourself when you are in school? _____

E. Lingua Angelica Extra:
Sing, "Dona Nobis Pacem" with the CD.
Write the Latin words once and translate.

_____

_____

_____

_____

_____

_____

_____

_____

Practical Latin

Deo Gratias   – Thanks be to God

Lesson – Nouns

Without nouns there would be no need for verbs. Who or what would do the
ACTION? You are a **noun**. Your house, your dog, and your pencil are nouns, too.

A **noun** is a *PERSON*, a *PLACE*, or a *THING.*

Our **Noun-Finder** asks 3 questions:

> 1.   Is it a PERSON?
> 2.   Is it a PLACE?
> 3.   Is it a THING?

If the answer is *yes* to just *one* of the questions, the word is a noun.

Example: girl
   Is it a **person**?   ✓ Yes! A girl is a person, so **girl** is a **noun**.

Example: flower
   Is it a **person**?   ☒ No, a flower is not a person.
   Is it a **place**?   ☒ No, a flower is not a place.
   Is it a **thing**?   ✓ Yes! A flower is a thing, so **flower** is a **noun**.

Example: jump
   Is it a **person**?   ☒ No, a jump is not a person.
   Is it a **place**?   ☒ No, a jump is not a place.
   Is it a **thing**?   ☒ No, jump is not a thing, so **jump** is **NOT** a **noun**.

Vocabulary

Notice the **a** ending on each of these Latin nouns below.

1.	regin**a**	queen
2.	stell**a**	star
3.	silv**a**	forest
4.	terr**a**	earth
5.	und**a**	wave
6.	vit**a**	life

Latin Prayers (The Doxology)

Gloria Patri,
et Filio, et Spiritui Sancto.
Sicut erat in principio,
et nunc, et semper,
et in saecula saeculorum. Amen.

– Glory be to the Father,
– Son, and Holy Spirit.
– As it was in the beginning,
– is now, and ever shall be,
– world without end. Amen.

Derivatives

regal	-- like a king or queen, befitting royalty (adj.)
stellar	-- having to do with a star, outstanding (adj.)
constellation	-- a group of stars that form a picture (n.)
Pennsylvania	-- a state of the North East U.S. (proper noun)
territory	-- area of land (n.)
undulating	-- wave-like motion (n.)
vital	-- extremely important (adj.)
vitamin	-- a natural substance that is essential to health (n.)

Review Questions

1. Practice saying all the vowel sounds in Latin.

2. Practice saying the six Latin consonant sounds from Lesson 2.

3. How do you say, "Stand up" (to many) in Latin? _____

4. How do you say, "Let us pray" in Latin? _____

5. How do you say, "Hello, students" (many) in Latin? _____

Lesson 6 Questions

1. A noun is a _____, _____, or _____.

2. List five nouns you can see right now. _____, _____,

_____   _____   _____

3. What are the three questions we use to see if a word is a noun?

1._____

2._____

3._____

4. In the Noun-Finder, how many questions have to be YES for a word to be a noun?

_____

5. What kind of noun are you: a person, place, or thing? _____

Translate

1. unda   _____

2. terra   _____

3. stella   _____

4. vita   _____

5. silva   _____

6. regina   _____

Speaking Latin --Listen to the Lesson 6 track on your Prima Latina CD--

☐ Say each vocabulary word and its meaning five times. Practice your pronunciation.

☐ Practice saying the Latin Prayer from Lesson 6, the Doxology, five times. Write it once with the English translation.

_____

☐ Say, "Deo Gratias" when you are thankful this week.

Write and Learn

Write each vocabulary word and its meaning twice.

1. _____   _____
   _____   _____

2. _____   _____
   _____   _____

3. _____   _____
   _____   _____

4. _____   _____
   _____   _____

5. _____   _____
   _____   _____

6. _____   _____
   _____   _____

Fun Practice

Draw a picture of your neighborhood. Label all of the nouns.

Practical Latin

Mea Culpa — my fault

Lesson – Latin Nouns

Like verbs, we can recognize **Latin nouns** in their dictionary forms by their endings. In Latin, there are five groups of nouns.
In the first group all of the nouns end in **A.**

English nouns are like English verbs; they can end in any letter. In the example below, notice that both of the Latin nouns end in **a,** but the endings for the English words are different.

Example:

Latin Noun	**English Noun**
aqu**a**	wate**r**
patri**a**	countr**y**

So again, in English, we have to decide if a word is a **noun** by *thinking* about it. But, in this book, we can decide if a **Latin** word is a **noun** by simply *looking* at it.

Vocabulary

Notice the **a** at the end of the Latin nouns below.

1. aqu**a**		water
2. cen**a**		dinner
3. coron**a**		crown
4. mens**a**		table
5. patri**a**		country

Latin Prayers (The Doxology)

Gloria Patri,
et Filio, et Spiritui Sancto.
Sicut erat in principio,
et nunc, et semper,
et in saecula saeculorum. Amen.

– Glory be to the Father,
– Son, and Holy Spirit.
– As it was in the beginning,
– is now, and ever shall be,
– world without end. Amen.

Derivatives

aquarium	-- a tank for keeping water animals (n.)
aquatic	-- relating to, or being in water (adj.)
coronation	-- the crowning of a king/queen (n.)
patriot	-- someone who loves his/her country (n.)
patriotic	-- showing a love for one's country (adj.)

Review Questions

1. What consonant is missing from the Latin alphabet? _____

2. In what letter do simple verbs end? _____

3. What does a **J** sound like in Latin? _____

4. What do we call verbs that have action but do not show it? _____

5. How many vowels are there in the alphabet? _____

Lesson 7 Questions

1. Name three ways to identify a noun.

   It is a _____, _____, or _____.

2. In what letter do many simple Latin nouns end? _____

Translate

1. mensa _____

2. patria _____

3. aqua _____

4. corona _____

5. cena _____

Speaking Latin --Listen to the Lesson 7 track on your Prima Latina CD--

☐ Say each vocabulary word and its meaning five times. Practice your pronunciation.

☐ Practice saying the Latin Prayers from Lessons 6 and 7, the Doxology, five times.

☐ Say, "mea culpa" whenever you make a mistake this week.

Write and Learn

Write each vocabulary word and its meaning twice.

1. _____   _____

   _____   _____

2. _____   _____

   _____   _____

3. _____   _____

   _____   _____

4. _____   _____

   _____   _____

5. _____   _____

   _____   _____

Fun Practice

Write a list (in English) of six nouns you see in the room.

Check ✔ person, place, or thing for each noun.

Noun	person, place, or thing		
_____	☐ person	☐ place	☐ thing
_____	☐ person	☐ place	☐ thing
_____	☐ person	☐ place	☐ thing
_____	☐ person	☐ place	☐ thing
_____	☐ person	☐ place	☐ thing
_____	☐ person	☐ place	☐ thing

Practical Latin

amicus	– friend
amici	– friends

Lesson – Derivatives

Derivatives are English words that come from Latin root words.
A derivative looks like its Latin root word and has a similar or related meaning.
You have been learning derivatives since lesson one!

Following are some **derivatives** for the vocabulary words in this book.
Notice the similarities in the spelling and meaning between the Latin root word and their
derivatives.

Latin Word	English Derivative	Translation
1. vita	<u>vita</u>min	life
	a vitamin is a natural substance necessary for life	
2. terra	<u>terr</u>itory	earth
	a territory is an area of land	
3. navigo	<u>navig</u>ate	I sail
	to navigate is to steer a ship or plane	
4. porto	<u>port</u>able	I carry
	portable is something able to be moved or carried	
5. oro	<u>or</u>al	I pray
	oral is having to do with the mouth	
6. laboro	<u>labo</u>ratory	I work
	a laboratory is a place where scientists work	
7. specto	<u>spect</u>ator	I look at
	a spectator is someone who watches an event	

Vocabulary

Consider the English **derivatives** of these words.

Latin Word	English Derivative	Translation
1. herba	herb	plant
2. injuria	injury	injury
3. femina	female, feminine	woman
4. nauta	nautical, navy	sailor
5. fortuna	fortune, fortunate	luck

Latin Prayers (The Doxology)

Gloria Patri,
et Filio, et Spiritui Sancto.

Sicut erat in principio,

et nunc, et semper,
et in saecula saeculorum. Amen.

– Glory be to the Father,
– Son, and Holy Spirit.

– As it was in the beginning,

– is now, and ever shall be,
– world without end. Amen.

Review Questions

1. What is an action word called? _____

2. Which of the two kinds of letters, vowel or consonant, is the letter **S**?

   _____

3. What is a person, place, or thing? _____

4. How do you say, "my fault" in Latin? _____

5. How do you say, "Thanks be to God" in Latin? _____

Lesson 8 Questions

1. What do you call an English word that has a similar meaning to, and spelling as,

   a Latin word? _____

2. What is a derivative of **nauta**? _____

3. What is a derivative of **herba**? _____

4. What is a derivative of **femina**? _____

5. What is a derivative of **fortuna**? _____

6. What is a derivative of **injuria**? _____

Translate

1. femina _____

2. fortuna _____

3. injuria _____

4. nauta _____

5. herba _____

Speaking Latin --Listen to the Lesson 8 track on your Prima Latina CD--

☐ Say each vocabulary word and its meaning five times. Practice your pronunciation.

☐ Tell your friends, "Hello" and, "Goodbye" in Latin all week. Use the Latin word for friend when you have the chance.

Write and Learn

Write each vocabulary word and its meaning twice. Write the derivatives next to the word each time.

	Word	Derivative	Translation
1.	_____	_____	_____
	_____	_____	_____
2.	_____	_____	_____
	_____	_____	_____
3.	_____	_____	_____
	_____	_____	_____
4.	_____	_____	_____
	_____	_____	_____
5.	_____	_____	_____
	_____	_____	_____

Fun Practice

Can you think of other derivatives for the Latin vocabulary words you have learned? On a separate sheet of paper, list the derivatives with the corresponding Latin word.

Practical Latin

Sedete   – Sit Down
                                          (to many)

Lesson – Numbers 1-5

This week we will learn the numbers one through five (1-5) in Latin.

Vocabulary

Numbers

1. unus	1 (one)
2. duo	2 (two)
3. tres	3 (three)
4. quattuor	4 (four)
5. quinque	5 (five)

Latin Prayers (The Doxology)

Gloria Patri,
et Filio, et Spiritui Sancto.
Sicut erat in principio,
et nunc, et semper,
et in saecula saeculorum. Amen.

– Glory be to the Father,
– Son, and Holy Spirit.
– As it was in the beginning,
– is now, and ever shall be,
– world without end. Amen.

Derivatives

unite	-- to join or make one (v.)
unicorn	-- a mythical creature with a one horn (n.)
dual	-- double (adj.)
tertiary	-- third (adj.)
trio	-- a group of three (n.)
quartet	-- a group of four (n.)
quarter	-- a fourth of something (n.)
quintuplets	-- five babies born at the same time from the same mother (n.)

Review Questions

Respond to the following questions in Latin.

1. How do you say, "Thanks be to God"? _____

2. What do you call a group of your playmates? _____

3. How do you say, "Hello, students"? _____

4. What is the opposite of, "Stand Up"? _____

Translate

1. quinque _____

2. duo _____

3. tres _____

4. quattuor _____

5. unus _____

Speaking Latin --Listen to the Lesson 9 track on your Prima Latina CD--

☐ Count from 1 to 5, five times. Practice your pronunciation.

☐ Practice saying the Latin Prayers from Lessons 6 through 9, the Doxology, five times.

☐ Say, "Sedete" each time you sit down this week.

Write and Learn

Write the words for numbers 1-5 in Latin five times each.

1. _____

2. _____

3. _____

4. _____

5. _____

Fun Practice

Draw a picture to illustrate each noun below.

Write a Latin description by each picture.

Note

In English, we add an **s** to make a noun plural.

In Latin, we add an **ae** to make the nouns you've learned plural.

(as you progress in Latin, you will learn several endings to make nouns plural)

Example: 4 moons – quattuor lun**ae**

4 Queens

5 Earths

Practical Latin

Anno Domini, A.D.   – In the Year of our Lord

Lesson – Numbers 6-10

Notice how some Latin numbers resemble the names of the months of our calendar.

Vocabulary

sex	6 (six)
septem	7 (seven)
octo	8 (eight)
novem	9 (nine)
decem	10 (ten)

Latin Prayers (The Doxology)

Gloria Patri,
et Filio, et Spiritui Sancto.
Sicut erat in principio,
et nunc, et semper,
et in saecula saeculorum. Amen.

– Glory be to the Father,
– Son, and Holy Spirit.
– As it was in the beginning,
– is now, and ever shall be,
– world without end. Amen.

Derivatives

semester -- historically a six-month term of school (15 to 18 weeks now) (n.)

September -- the seventh month of the Roman calendar (n.)

October -- the eighth month of the Roman calendar (n.)

octagon -- an eight-sided figure (n.)

November -- the ninth month of the Roman calendar (n.)

December -- the tenth month of the Roman calendar (n.)

decimal -- based on the number 10 (adj.)

Review Questions

Use the Latin numbers 1-10 to answer the following questions.

1. How old are you?_____

2. How many ears do you have?_____

3. How many siblings do you have? _____ (use "nullus" for none)

4. How many toes do you have?_____

5. How many ice cream scoops do you want? _____

Lesson 10 Questions

What Latin number corresponds with the following months?

1. November _____

2. October _____

3. September _____

4. December _____

Speaking Latin --Listen to the Lesson 10 track on your Prima Latina CD--

☐ Say the numbers 1 through 10 in Latin five times. Practice your pronunciation.

☐ Practice saying the entire Doxology five times.

Write and Learn

1. Write the numbers 1 through 5 in Latin three times. Write the number next to the word.

_____

_____

_____

_____

_____

Write and Learn

1. Write the numbers 6 through 10 in Latin five times. Write the number next to the word.

6. _____

7. _____

8. _____

9. _____

10. _____

2. Write the entire Doxology one time.

_____

_____

_____

_____

_____

3. Write down the birthdays of five special people. Write **A.D.** at the end of each to signify that the person was born after the birth of Christ.

_____   _____

_____   _____

_____

Fun Practice

Look around your house and count how many of the following items you have.
Write the quantity in Latin.

1. televisions _____   5. bicycles _____

2. brooms _____   6. couches _____

3. bedrooms _____   7. fishing poles _____

4. toothbrushes _____   8. automobiles _____

Vocabulary

Nouns

regina	queen
stella	star
silva	forest
terra	earth
unda	wave
aqua	water
cena	dinner
corona	crown
mensa	table
patria	country
herba	plant
injuria	injury
femina	woman
nauta	sailor
fortuna	luck
vita	life

Numbers

unus	one
duo	two
tres	three
quattuor	four
quinque	five
sex	six
septem	seven
octo	eight
novem	nine
decem	ten

> **Latin Song--** "Christus Vincit"
> Christus Vincit--Christ conquers
> Christus Regnat--Christ reigns
> Christus Imperat--Christ rules

Practical Latin

Deo gratias	Thanks be to God
mea culpa	my fault
amicus	friend
amici	friends
Sedete	Sit down (to many)
Anno Domini (A.D.)	In the year of our Lord

Latin Prayers – The Doxology

Gloria Patri,	Glory be to the Father,
et Filio, et Spiritui Sancto.	Son, and Holy Spirit.
Sicut erat in principio,	As it was in the beginning,
et nunc, et semper,	is now, and ever shall be,
et in saecula saeculorum. Amen.	world without end. Amen.

A. Copy all vocabulary words and translate.

Extra: Write one derivative next to each word.

	Word	Translation	Derivative
1.			
2.			
3.			
4.			
5.			
6.			
7.			
8.			
9.			
10.			
11.			
12.			
13.			
14.			
15.			
16.			
17.			
18.			
19.			
20.			
21.			
22.			
23.			
24.			
25.			
26.			

B. Answer the following questions.

    1. What part of speech is a person, place, or thing? _____

    2. In what letter do nouns you have learned end? _____

    3. Name four months that are derivatives of Latin numbers. _____

    _____, _____, _____

C. Practice saying the Doxology completely.
Say it five times from memory. Write it once.

_____

_____

_____

_____

_____

D. Answer the following questions in Latin.

    1. How could you end a prayer? _____

    2. What do you call people you like? _____

    3. What do you do when you say the Pledge of Allegiance? _____

    4. What do you say when you make a mistake and take responsibility for it?

    _____

    5. What is the complete way to write what year this is? _____

    _____

    (Hint: is it before or after the birth of Christ?)

E. Lingua Angelica Extra: Sing, "Christus Vincit" with the CD.
Write the Latin words once and translate.

_____

_____

_____

Practical Latin

Veni, vidi, vici

– I came, I saw, I conquered. (Julius Caesar)

Lesson – Proper Nouns

A **proper noun** is a noun that names a *specific* person, place, or thing.

(Nouns that are not **proper nouns** are called "common nouns." The nouns we have learned about so far are common nouns.)

Example: **girl**
The noun **girl** can refer to any girl. **Girl** is a **common noun**.

The noun **Sylvia** refers only to the girl named Sylvia.
Sylvia is a **proper noun**.

An easy way to recognize a proper noun is by a **CAPITAL LETTER** for the first letter of the word.

Note: a common noun may have a capital first letter if it is at the beginning of a sentence, but, if it doesn't refer to a specific person, place, or thing, it is still a common noun.

Let's think of some other noun/proper noun pairs.

Common Noun	**Proper Noun**
country	Italy
state	Tennessee
girl	Sarah Hughes
boy	Julius Caesar
book	*Prima Latina*
game	Monopoly

54

Vocabulary

Notice the capital letters.

1. Roma	Rome
2. Italia	Italy
3. Maria	Mary
4. Marcus	Marcus
5. Hispania	Spain

Latin Prayers (The Table Blessing)

Benedic, Domine, nos
et haec Tua dona
quae de Tua largitate
sumus sumpturi.
Per Christum Dominum nostrum. Amen.

-- Bless us, O Lord,
-- and these Your gifts
-- which from Your bounty
-- we are about to receive.
-- through Christ our Lord. Amen.

Derivatives

Roman   -- having to do with Rome (adj.)

Italian   -- having to do with Italy (adj.)

Spanish   -- having to do with Spain (adj.)

Hispanic   -- a Latin-American person who lives in the U.S. (n.)

Review Questions

What kind of word is each of the following: noun, verb, or proper noun?

1. bird   _____

2. jump   _____

3. Rome   _____

4. love   _____

5. Mary   _____

Lesson 11 Questions

1. A noun that names a specific person, place, or thing is called a _____ noun.

2. List three Latin proper nouns you know. _____,_____,_____

3. What is an easy way to recognize a proper noun? _____

4. Write a proper noun for each of the following nouns.

   boy   _____

   restaurant _____

   book   _____

   city   _____

Translate

1. Roma   _____

2. Maria   _____

3. Hispania   _____

4. Marcus   _____

5. Italia   _____

Speaking Latin   --Listen to the Lesson 11 track on your Prima Latina CD--

☐ Say each vocabulary word and its meaning five times. Practice your pronunciation.

☐ Practice saying the Practical Latin saying, "Veni, vidi, vici" each time you accomplish something difficult.

☐ Practice saying the Latin Prayer from Lesson 11, the Table Blessing, before your mealtime prayer.

Write and Learn

1. Write each vocabulary word and its meaning twice.

1. _____   _____

     _____   _____

2. _____   _____

     _____   _____

3. _____   _____

     _____   _____

4. _____   _____

     _____   _____

5. _____   _____

     _____   _____

Fun Practice

Write a list of ten common nouns. Match each with an appropriate proper noun.

	Common Noun	**Proper Noun**
Example	city	Atlanta
1.	_____	_____
2.	_____	_____
3.	_____	_____
4.	_____	_____
5.	_____	_____
6.	_____	_____
7.	_____	_____
8.	_____	_____
9.	_____	_____
10.	_____	_____

Practical Latin

Quo vadis?   – Where are you going?

Lesson – Prepositions

Prepositions are words that show a RELATIONSHIP between two words.
It helps to first think of **prepositions** as words that show the location or *position* of something. This is easy to remember because the word **position** is in the word pre**position**.

Examples of **prepositions** are:

under	on
in	above
out of	between
with	by

For example, think of a noun–let's say, "desk".
Now, let's think of *where the desk is...*

Is the desk *under* the roof?
Is it *on* the floor?
Is it flying *in* the air?
Is it *by* the wall?

The benefit of **prepositions** is that they help us know *where the desk is located.*

Vocabulary

These are Latin **prepositions.**

1. inter		between
2. sub		under
3. supra		above
4. ex		out of
5. contra		against

Latin Prayers (The Table Blessing)

Benedic, Domine, nos	-- Bless us, O Lord,
et haec Tua dona	**-- and these Your gifts**
quae de Tua largitate	-- which from Your bounty
sumus sumpturi.	-- we are about to receive.
Per Christum Dominum nostrum. Amen.	-- Through Christ our Lord. Amen.

Derivatives

interrupt	-- to make a break in conversation or action (v.)
intermediate	-- in the middle (adj.)
submarine	-- underwater ship (n.)
subway	-- underground railway (n.)
superb	-- above average, excellent (adj.)
exit	-- a way out (n.)
extraordinary	-- out of the ordinary, very unusual (adj.)
contrary	-- opposite or different (adj.)
contrast	-- to compare unlike things (v.)

Review Questions

Answer the following questions in English.

1. What is a word that shows action called? _____

2. Who said, "Veni, vidi, vici"? _____

3. What is a specific person, place, or thing? _____

4. What is an English word with a similar spelling and meaning to a Latin word?

   _____

Lesson 12 Exercises

Use an English preposition in the vocabulary list to write a sentence describing the location of the following nouns. You decide where each item is located.

Example: The girl is *in* the house.

1. table   _____

2. moon   _____

3. toga   _____

4. queen   _____

5. boy   _____

Translate

1. supra   _____

2. contra   _____

3. inter   _____

4. sub   _____

5. ex   _____

Speaking Latin --Listen to the Lesson 12 track on your Prima Latina CD--

☐ Say each vocabulary word and its meaning five times. Practice your pronunciation.

☐ Say the Latin Prayers from Lessons 11 and 12, the Table Blessing, before your mealtime prayer.

☐ When you change locations this week, use Latin prepositions to identify where you are.

Write and Learn

1. Write each vocabulary word and its meaning three times.

Word	Meaning
1. _____	_____
_____	_____
2. _____	_____
_____	_____
3. _____	_____
_____	_____
4. _____	_____
_____	_____
5. _____	_____
_____	_____

Fun Practice

Draw a picture of a school scene on another sheet of paper. Describe the nouns in your picture using prepositions. Example: The floor is under the desk.

_____

_____

_____

_____

_____

Practical Latin

alma mater   – nurturing mother

Lesson – Pronouns

A **pronoun** is a word that *replaces* a noun or **pronoun**.

It *refers* to a person, place, or thing without actually saying a name.

English **pronouns** include:

I	we
you (s.)	you (pl.)
he	they
she	
it	

Example: Let's talk about Mary and her dog.

> We could say, **Mary** is pretty. **Mary** is 8 years old.
> **Mary** has a dog. **Mary's dog** has red hair.

But it is easier to take a break from using her name and use **pronouns**.

> Mary is pretty. **She** is 8 years old. **She** has a dog.
> **It** has red hair.

Pronoun letters are at the end of **verbs** in Latin.

You will learn later that using pronoun letters is the first step in *conjugating* verbs.

Singular (s.) and Plural (pl.)

Notice that *"you"* is listed twice in the English pronouns, once as singular (s.) and once as plural (pl.). *"You"* is tricky because it can be singular or plural. The pronoun *"you"* is singular or plural based on who is being addressed.

Singular *"you"* is addressed to one person. If Mary's mom tells her:

> *"You* have homework to do." She is addressing a single person, Mary.

Plural *"you"* is addressed to more than one person. If Mary's teacher tells her class:

> *"You* have homework to do." She is talking to a group of people, the class.

Grammar

These are **verb endings** (**pronoun letters**) in Latin. They go on the end of verbs and tell us which pronoun goes with a Latin verb. You will learn how to use these in the chapter on conjugating verbs. For now, just memorize the pronoun letters.

1. **o**	I
2. **s**	you
3. **t**	he, she, it
4. **mus**	we
5. **tis**	you (plural)
6. **nt**	they

Latin Prayers (The Table Blessing)

Benedic, Domine, nos — -- Bless us, O Lord,
et haec Tua dona — -- and these Your gifts
quae de Tua largitate — **-- which from Your bounty**
sumus sumpturi. — -- we are about to receive.
Per Christum Dominum nostrum. Amen. — -- Through Christ our Lord. Amen.

Review Questions

Answer the following questions in English.

1. What is an action word called? _____

2. What is a specific noun called? _____

3. What kind of word shows relationship? _____

4. What is a word that replaces a noun? _____

5. What letter is missing from the Latin alphabet? _____

Lesson 13 Questions

Write the pronoun that would best replace the underlined words in the following sentences.

1. The boy climbed a tree. _____

2. The girls ran across the field. _____

3. My family goes to church. _____

4. My desk is in the classroom. _____

5. Suzie drives a car. _____

Translate

What Latin verb endings (pronoun letters) correspond to the following pronouns?

1. you (singular) _____

2. I   _____

3. we   _____

4. he, she, it   _____

5. they   _____

6. you (plural) _____

Speaking Latin --Listen to the Lesson 13 track on your Prima Latina CD--

☐ Say each verb ending and its corresponding pronoun five times.

Write and Learn

Write each verb ending and its corresponding pronoun twice.

1. _____   _____
   _____   _____

2. _____   _____
   _____   _____

3. _____   _____
   _____   _____

4. _____   _____
   _____   _____

5. _____   _____
   _____   _____

6. _____   _____
   _____   _____

Fun Practice

Write a song or poem to help you remember the verb endings.

_____

_____

_____

_____

_____

_____

_____

Practical Latin

Stupor Mundi   – wonder of the world

Lesson – Adjectives

Adjectives are words used to *modify* (or change) nouns or pronouns.
Adjectives *DESCRIBE* a person, place or thing.
They can be colors, sizes, numbers, or shapes, for example.

Adjectives modify nouns and pronouns and make them more interesting.
For example, think of a city. What kind of a city is it?
The words you use to describe it are **adjectives**.

Below, the adjectives are in bold print.

Is it **hot**?

Is it **big**?

Is it **old**?

Is it **crowded**?

Now, think of your room. Think of some **adjectives** to describe it.

What color is it?

What shape is it?

How big is it?

Vocabulary

Here are some Latin adjectives.

1. altus	high, deep
2. multus	much, many
3. bonus	good
4. longus	long
5. novus	new

Latin Prayers (The Table Blessing)

Benedic, Domine, nos — Bless us, O Lord,
et haec Tua dona — and these Your gifts
quae de Tua largitate — which from Your bounty
sumus sumpturi. **-- we are about to receive.**
Per Christum Dominum nostrum. Amen. -- Through Christ our Lord. Amen.

Derivatives

altitude	-- height (n.)
multiply	-- to increase (v.)
bonus	-- something extra (n.)
longitude	-- imaginary lines that run vertically on a globe (n.)
innovation	-- a new invention (n.)
novice	-- beginner (n.)
novel	-- new and unusual (adj.)

Review Questions

1. Practice saying the Sanctus from memory.
2. Write the Sanctus in full and translate.

_____

_____

_____

_____

_____

_____

Lesson 14 Questions

Answer the following questions in English.

1. What is another word for "modify"? _____

2. What do adjectives do? _____

3. What two kinds of words do adjectives modify? _____

4. List three adjectives that describe you. _____, _____, _____.

5. List three adjectives that describe your house. _____ ,

_____ _____

Translate

1. longus _____

2. bonus _____

3. novus _____

4. altus _____

5. multus _____

Speaking Latin --Listen to the Lesson 14 track on your Prima Latina Cd--

☐ Say the vocabulary words five times. Practice your pronunciation.

☐ Practice saying "Wonder of the World" in Latin.

Write and Learn

Write each vocabulary word and its meaning twice.

1. _____   _____
   _____   _____

2. _____   _____
   _____   _____

3. _____   _____
   _____   _____

4. _____   _____
   _____   _____

5. _____   _____

Fun Practice

Circle the words that may be adjectives.

blue	run	jump	in	tree
two	square	book	new	high
car	good	long	boy	Mary

Practical Latin

Nunc aut numquam   – Now or never

Lesson – Adverbs

Adverbs are words that modify (or change) **VERBS**. This is easy to remember because the word **VERB** is in the word AD**VERB.**

Adverbs describe **how, where, when,** or **why** a verb happens.
Many English **adverbs** can be identified by the letters **ly** at the end.

For example, let's choose a verb: walk.
 Now, let's think of the different ways you can walk.
 You may want to practice these.

 You can:

walk quick*ly*	walk slow*ly*
walk loud*ly*	walk quiet*ly*
walk proud*ly*	walk sad*ly*

All the words above are **adverbs.** See how they modify or change the verb *walk*?

Adverbs can also tell *when* a verb happens.

Examples of this kind of **adverb** are:

now	never
often	always

Now, let's think of how these adverbs can modify walk
You can:

walk *now*	*never* walk
walk *often*	*always* walk

Vocabulary

Here are some Latin **adverbs**.

1.	clam	secretly
2.	numquam	never
3.	nunc	now
4.	saepe	often
5.	semper	always

Latin Prayers (The Table Blessing)

Benedic, Domine, nos — -- Bless us, O Lord,
et haec Tua dona — -- and these Your gifts
quae de Tua largitate — -- which from Your bounty
sumus sumpturi. — -- we are about to receive.

Per Christum Dominum nostrum. Amen. — **-- Through Christ our Lord. Amen.**

Review Questions

Answer the following questions in Latin.

1. What is Julius Caesar's most famous quote? _____

2. How do you say, "Where are you going?" _____

3. How do you say, "nurturing mother" in Latin? _____

4. What is the opposite of "Surgite"? _____

Lesson 15 Questions

1. What kinds of words do adverbs change or modify? _____

2. What is an easy way to remember what kind of word adverbs change? _____

   _____

3. Name four things an adverb tells you. _____

4. What is an easy way to recognize some English adverbs? _____

   _____

Translate

1. saepe   _____

2. semper   _____

3. nunc   _____

4. clam   _____

5. numquam   _____

Speaking Latin   --Listen to the Lesson 15 track on your Prima Latina CD--

☐ Say each vocabulary word and its meaning five times. Practice your
  pronunciation.

☐ Say the Table Blessing in full before your meals this week.

☐ Practice saying "Now or Never" in Latin when there is something you need to finish.

Write and Learn

1. Write each vocabulary word and its meaning twice.

1. _____   _____

   _____   _____

2. _____   _____

   _____   _____

3. _____   _____

   _____   _____

4. _____   _____

   _____   _____

5. _____   _____

   _____   _____

2. Write the Table Blessing once in Latin. Recite it from memory in English

_____

_____

_____

_____

_____

Fun Practice

Decide if the words below are adjectives or adverbs. Check ✔ either "adjective" or "adverb" next to each word.

soon	☐ adjective	☐ adverb	always	☐ adjective	☐ adverb
quietly	☐ adjective	☐ adverb	cold	☐ adjective	☐ adverb
purple	☐ adjective	☐ adverb	quickly	☐ adjective	☐ adverb
big	☐ adjective	☐ adverb	small	☐ adjective	☐ adverb
slowly	☐ adjective	☐ adverb	often	☐ adjective	☐ adverb

Vocabulary and Grammar

Proper Nouns

Roma	Rome
Italia	Italy
Maria	Mary
Marcus	Mark
Hispania	Spain

Prepositions

inter	between
sub	under
supra	above
ex	out of
contra	against

Adjectives

altus	high, deep
bonus	good
multus	much
longus	long
novus	new

Pronouns/Verb Endings

o	I
s	you
t	he, she, it
mus	we
tis	you (plural)
nt	they

Adverbs

clam	secretly
numquam	never
nunc	now
saepe	often
semper	always

> **Latin Song**--Refrain of "Adeste Fideles"
> Venite adoremus--O come let us adore Him,
> Venite adoremus--O come let us adore Him,
> Venite adoremus--O come let us adore Him,
> Dominum--Christ the Lord.

Practical Latin

Veni, vidi, vici	I came, I saw, I conquered.
Quo vadis?	Where are you going?
alma mater	nurturing mother
stupor mundi	wonder of the world
nunc aut numquam	now or never

Latin Prayers - The Table Blessing

Benedic, Domine, nos	Bless us, O Lord,
et haec Tua dona	and these Your gifts
quae de Tua largitate	which from Your bounty
sumus sumpturi.	we are about to receive.
Per Christum Dominum nostrum. Amen.	Through Christ our Lord. Amen.

A. Copy all vocabulary words and translate.

Extra: Write one derivative next to each word.

	Word	**Translation**	**Derivative**
1.	_____	_____	_____
2.	_____	_____	_____
3.	_____	_____	_____
4.	_____	_____	_____
5.	_____	_____	_____
6.	_____	_____	_____
7.	_____	_____	_____
8.	_____	_____	_____
9.	_____	_____	_____
10.	_____	_____	_____
11.	_____	_____	_____
12.	_____	_____	_____
13.	_____	_____	_____
14.	_____	_____	_____
15.	_____	_____	_____
16.	_____	_____	_____
17.	_____	_____	_____
18.	_____	_____	_____
19.	_____	_____	_____
20.	_____	_____	_____
21.	_____	_____	_____
22.	_____	_____	_____
23.	_____	_____	_____
24.	_____	_____	_____
25.	_____	_____	_____
26.	_____	_____	_____

B. *Answer the following questions.*

1. What is a word that names a specific person, place or thing? _____

2. What part of speech shows relationship and location? _____

3. What part of speech describes a noun or pronoun? _____

4. What part of speech describes a verb? _____

C. *Practice saying the Table Blessing completely.*
Say it three times in Latin and three times in English from memory.

Benedic, Domine, nos   – Bless us, O Lord,
et haec Tua dona   – and these your gifts
quae de Tua largitate   – which from your bounty
sumus sumpturi.   – we are about to receive.
Per Christum Dominum nostrum. Amen.   – Through Christ our Lord. Amen

D. *Fill in blanks in Latin. -- be sure to review your Latin Sayings --*

1. What can you say when you accomplish something hard? _____

2. What is the Latin saying for, "nurturing mother"? _____

3. What can you say when you must get something finished? _____

4. What can you call something beautiful, like a rainbow? _____

5. How do you ask where someone is going? _____

E. *Lingua Angelica Extra: Sing the Refrain of "Adeste Fideles" with the CD. Write the Latin words once and translate.*

_____

_____

_____

_____

_____

_____

Practical Latin

Semper Fidelis

– Always Faithful
(Marine Corps motto)

Lesson – Constellations

Constellations are groups of stars that form pictures in the sky. They often have fantastic myths created by the very early Greek and Roman civilizations to explain them. Scientists and sailors use constellations to map the sky.

Pictures of the Constellations

Aquarius - water carrier
Aquarius, or Ganymede, was the cupbearer to the gods

Aries - ram
This ram may have been the one whose golden fleece was the object of Jason's quest

Cancer - crab
In his second labor, Hercules was attacked by this giant crab sent by Hera

Capricorn - goat
Pan changed himself into a goat with a fish's tail

Gemini - twins
Zeus placed the Gemini twins, Castor and Pollux, together in the sky so they would never be separated again

Virgo - maiden, virgin
The goddess of justice who believed in people

Vocabulary

Here are the names of some constellations.

1. Aquarius	water carrier
2. Aries	ram
3. Cancer	crab
4. Capricorn	goat
5. Gemini	twins
6. Virgo	maiden, virgin

Latin Prayers (The Our Father or Lord's Prayer)

Pater Noster qui es in Caelis   – Our Father who is in Heaven

Review Questions

Answer the following questions in English.

1. What do you call words that modify verbs? _____

2. In what letter do simple Latin verbs end? _____

3. In what letter do nouns in our first group end? _____

4. What do you call a word that shows a relationship or location? _____

5. What do you call a word that describes a noun? _____

Lesson 16 Questions

1. What is a constellation? _____

2. Who named them and told stories to explain them? _____

3. Where can you see a constellation? _____

Translate

	Latin	English
	_____	_____
	_____	_____
	_____	_____
	_____	_____
	_____	_____
	_____	_____

Speaking Latin --Listen to the Lesson 16 track on your Prima Latina Cd--

☐ Say each vocabulary word and its meaning five times. Practice your pronunciation.

☐ Look for bumper stickers with "Semper Fidelis" or "Semper Fi" on them this week. Say the Marine Corps motto when when you see it.

Write and Learn

Write each vocabulary word and its meaning twice.

1. _____   _____
   _____   _____

2. _____   _____
   _____   _____

3. _____   _____
   _____   _____

4. _____   _____
   _____   _____

5. _____   _____
   _____   _____

6. _____   _____
   _____   _____

Fun Practice

Look in a science book to see pictures of the constellations. Draw and label the pictures you find.

Practical Latin

Repetite

– Repeat
(to many)

Lesson – More Constellations

Note the short mythical stories beneath each constellation. A myth is a traditional, ancient tale about supernatural beings or heros.

Pictures of the Constellations

Leo - lion
The lion Hercules fought for three days and three nights

Libra - scales of justics
Scales used to weigh good and evil

Pisces - fish
Aphrodite and Eros changed themselves into fish to escape a monster

Sagittarius - archer
The brave and wise centaur Chiron, who tutored Achilles, Hercules, and Asclepius

Scorpio - scorpion
Scorpio tried to kill the hunter Orion

Taurus - bull
Zeus changed himself into a bull to woo Europa

Vocabulary

Here are names of more constellations.

1. Leo	lion
2. Libra	scales of justice
3. Pisces	fish
4. Sagittarius	archer
5. Scorpio	scorpion
6. Taurus	bull

Latin Prayers (The Our Father or Lord's Prayer)

Sanctificetur nomen Tuum — Hallowed be Your name

Review Questions

1. Practice saying the Table Blessing.

2. Write the Table Blessing in full and translate.

_____

_____

_____

_____

_____

_____

_____

Translate

	Latin	English
	_____	_____
	_____	_____
	_____	_____
	_____	_____
	_____	_____
	_____	_____

Speaking Latin --Listen to the Lesson 17 track on your Prima Latina CD--

☐ Say each vocabulary word and its meaning five times. Practice your pronunciation.

☐ Politely say, "Repeat" in Latin this week when you need someone to repeat what they have said.

Write and Learn

Write each vocabulary word and its meaning twice.

1. _____   _____
   _____   _____

2. _____   _____
   _____   _____

3. _____   _____
   _____   _____

4. _____   _____
   _____   _____

5. _____   _____
   _____   _____

6. _____   _____
   _____   _____

Fun Practice

Look in a science book to see pictures of this week's constellations. On a separate piece of paper, draw and label the pictures you find.

Practical Latin

Quid agis?   – How are you?

Lesson – To Be Verb

The verb *to be* is the most common verb in any language. The *to be* verb shows existence, not action. This verb explains how we are, not how we act.

For example:
> I **am** a girl.
> You **are** tall.
> She **is** pretty.
> He **is** short.
> We **are** a family.
> They **are** happy.

Notice there are no other verbs in these sentences.
The words *is, am, are* take the place of an action or invisible verb.

Below are all the English forms of the *to be* verb in the present tense.

Singular		*Plural*	
I	am	we	are
you (s.)	are	you (pl.)	are
he, she, it	is	they	are

In Latin, the *to be* verb is irregular. If you look carefully at the *to be* verb, you will notice later that the endings resemble Latin verb endings.

Vocabulary

Notice the highlighted endings.

1.	sum	I am
2.	es	you (s.) are
3.	est	he, she, it is
4.	sumus	we are
5.	estis	you (pl.) are
6.	sunt	they are

Latin Prayers (The Our Father or Lord's Prayer)

Adveniat regnum Tuum   – May Your kingdom come

Review Questions

Answer the following questions in Latin.

1. What do you call your friends?_____

2. What does "A.D." mean? _____

3. What is the Marine Corps motto? _____

4. How do you say, "Repeat" in Latin?_____

5. How do you say, "Goodbye, Teacher" (male) in Latin? _____

Lesson 18 Questions

1. What is the most common verb in any language? _____

2. What does the *to be* verb show? _____

Translate

Check ✓ whether each verb is singular or plural.

1. estis _____ ☐ singular ☐ plural

2. es _____ ☐ singular ☐ plural

3. sunt _____ ☐ singular ☐ plural

4. sum _____ ☐ singular ☐ plural

5. sumus _____ ☐ singular ☐ plural

6. est _____ ☐ singular ☐ plural

Notes

Speaking Latin --Listen to the Lesson 18 track on your Prima Latina CD--

☐ Say each vocabulary word and its meaning five times. Practice your pronunciation.

☐ Ask your family and friends, "How are you?" in Latin this week.

Write and Learn

1. Write each vocabulary word and its meaning twice.

1. _____   _____
   _____   _____

2. _____   _____
   _____   _____

3. _____   _____
   _____   _____

4. _____   _____
   _____   _____

5. _____   _____
   _____   _____

6. _____   _____
   _____   _____

Fun Practice

Find your favorite storybook. Read the first three pages and count how many times you see the *to be* verb in the present tense. Look for the words **is, am, are.**

Practical Latin

      Satis bene   – very well

Lesson – To Be Able To / I Can

Sometimes we like to talk about the things we are **able to do**, the things we **can** do.

    For instance, here are some of the things I **can** do:

      I **can** swim.

      I **am able to** ride a bike.

      I **can** sing.

      I **am able to** play the flute.

    Other examples:

      You **are able** to run.

      He **is able** to ski.

      She **can** ride horses.

      We **are able** to hear.

      They **are able** to dance.

* It is important not to confuse the word **can** with the word **may**.

Can is used when you are capable.

May is used when you are allowed.

In Latin there is a special **I can** verb.

Notice the similarities with the *to be* verb from Lesson 18.

Vocabulary

Here are the forms of **to be able to**.

1. possum	I can
2. potes	you (s.) can
3. potest	he, she, it can
4. possumus	we can
5. potestis	you (pl.) can
6. possunt	they can

Latin Prayers (The Our Father or Lord's Prayer)

Fiat voluntas Tua   – Your will be done

Derivatives

possible   -- can be (adj.)

Review Questions

1. Practice saying the Doxology once from memory.

2. Write the Doxology once for practice.

_____

_____

_____

_____

_____

Lesson 19 Questions

1. What do all the *I can* verbs have in common? _____

2. What verb is present in all the *I can* verbs? _____

Translate

Check ✓ whether each verb is singular or plural.

1. possumus   _____   ☐ singular ☐ plural

2. potestis   _____   ☐ singular ☐ plural

3. potes   _____   ☐ singular ☐ plural

4. possum   _____   ☐ singular ☐ plural

5. potest   _____   ☐ singular ☐ plural

6. possunt   _____   ☐ singular ☐ plural

Speaking Latin --Listen to the Lesson 19 track on your Prima Latina CD--

☐ Say each vocabulary word and its meaning five times. Practice your pronunciation.

☐ When people ask how you are this week, answer in Latin.

(And then in English to be polite.)

Write and Learn

1. Write each vocabulary word and its meaning twice.

    1. _____   _____

       _____   _____

    2. _____   _____

       _____   _____

    3. _____   _____

       _____   _____

    4. _____   _____

       _____   _____

    5. _____   _____

       _____   _____

    6. _____   _____

       _____   _____

Fun Practice

Make a list of 10 things you CAN do.

    1. _____   6. _____

    2. _____   7. _____

    3. _____   8. _____

    4. _____   9. _____

    5. _____   10. _____

Practical Latin

Romanus civis sum — I am a citizen of Rome

Lesson – Future Tense

Everything we have talked about so far has been in the **present tense**.
Present tense means that something is happening right now.

> For example:
>> I learn. *OR*   I am learning.
>> I sit. *OR* I am sitting.
>> I write. *OR* I am writing.

Sometimes, there are things we look forward to happening in the **future**.
In English, we add the word *will* to indicate something will happen
in the **future**.

> For example:
>> I <u>will</u> go on vacation this summer.
>> I <u>will</u> graduate from high school in 10 years.
>> I <u>will</u> go to the park tomorrow.

In Latin, instead of adding the extra word *will*, we add a special ending to our verbs.

On the following page are the **Future Tense Verb Endings.**
They are added to verbs, not used alone.
Again, notice the similarities with the other verb endings.

Grammar

Below are the future tense verb endings. They are added to verbs to form future
tense. An example is voca**bo** - I will call.
Notice the highlighted endings.

1. b**o**	I will
2. bi**s**	you will
3. bi**t**	he, she, or it will
4. bi**mus**	we will
5. bi**tis**	you (pl.) will
6. bu**nt**	they will

Latin Prayers (The Our Father or Lord's Prayer)

Sicut in Caelo et in terra   – As in Heaven and on earth

Review Questions

1. What does a **J** sound like in Latin? _____

2. What are the letters **A, E, I, O, U** called? _____

3. How many letters are in the Latin alphabet? _____

4. What does a Latin **E** sound like? _____

5. What does a Latin **I** sound like? _____

Lesson 20 Questions

1. What tense describes things that are happening right now? _____

2. What tense describes things that are going to happen? _____

3. What word do we add to sentences in English to show future tense? _____

4. How are future tense endings similar to all other verb endings we have learned? __

   _____

Speaking Latin   --Listen to the Lesson 20 track on your Prima Latina CD-- _____

☐ Say each future tense verb ending and its meaning five times. Practice your
pronunciation.

Notes

Write and Learn

1. Write each future tense ending and its meaning twice.

    1. _____   _____

       _____   _____

    2. _____   _____

       _____   _____

    3. _____   _____

       _____   _____

    4. _____   _____

       _____   _____

    5. _____   _____

       _____   _____

    6. _____   _____

       _____   _____

2. Write the Latin Prayers from Lessons 16 through 20, the Lord's Prayer, and translate.

    _____

    _____

    _____

    _____

    _____

Fun Practice

Write a list of ten things you will do in the future.

1. _____   6. _____

2. _____   7. _____

3. _____   8. _____

4. _____   9. _____

5. _____   10. _____

Vocabulary

Aquarius	water carrier
Aries	ram
Cancer	crab
Capricorn	goat
Gemini	twins
Virgo	maiden
Leo	lion
Libra	scales
Pisces	fish
Sagittarius	archer
Scorpio	scorpion
Taurus	bull

Grammar

To Be Verb

sum	I am
es	you are
est	he, she, it is
sumus	we are
estis	you (pl.) are
sunt	they are

To Be Able/Can Verb

possum	I can
potes	you can
potest	he, she, it can
possumus	we can
potestis	you (pl.) can
possunt	they can

Future Tense Endings

bo	I will
bis	you will
bit	he, she, it will
bimus	we will
bitis	you (pl.) will
bunt	they will

> **Latin Song--** Refrain of
> "Resonet in Laudibus"
> Gaudete--Rejoice!
> Gaudete--Rejoice!

Practical Latin

Semper Fidelis	Always Faithful
repetite	repeat
Quid agis?	How are you?
Satis bene	very well
Romanus civis sum	I am a citizen of Rome

Latin Prayers (The Our Father or Lord's Prayer)

Pater Noster, qui es in caelis,	Our Father, who is in heaven,
sanctificetur nomen Tuum.	hallowed be Your name.
Adveniat regnum Tuum.	Your kingdom come.
Fiat voluntas Tua,	Your will be done,
sicut in Caelo et in terra.	on earth as it is in heaven.

A. Copy all vocabulary words and translate.

Extra: Write one derivative next to each word.

Word	Derivative	Translation
1.		
2.		
3.		
4.		
5.		
6.		
7.		
8.		
9.		
10.		
11.		
12.		
13.		
14.		
15.		
16.		
17.		
18.		
19.		
20.		
21.		
22.		
23.		
24.		
25.		
26.		
27.		
28.		
29.		
30.		

B. Answer the following questions.

1. What are groups of stars in the sky called? _____

2. What is the most common verb? _____

3. What tense describes things that *will* happen? _____

4. What tense describes things that are happening? _____

5. What is a word that names a specific person, place, or thing? _____

6. What part of speech shows relationship and/or location? _____

7. What part of speech describes a noun or pronoun? _____

8. What part of speech describes a verb? _____

C. Practice saying the first half of the Lord's Prayer. Write it & translate.

_____

_____

_____

_____

_____

D. Translate.

1. Always Faithful _____

2. Quid agis? _____

3. nurturing mother _____

4. wonder of the world _____

5. Thanks be to God _____

6. my fault _____

7. In the Year of our Lord _____

8. Oremus _____

E. Lingua Angelica Extra:

Sing the Refrain of, "Resonet in Laudibus" with the CD.
Write the Latin words once and translate.

_____

_____

_____

_____

_____

_____

Notes

_____

_____

_____

_____

_____

_____

_____

_____

_____

_____

_____

_____

_____

_____

_____

_____

Practical Latin

E pluribus unum   – One out of many

Lesson – Conjunctions

Sicut, et, and sed, in today's vocabulary list are **conjunctions**.
A conjunction is a word that joins words or groups of words.

Examples:

I like to swim **and** I like to run.

You are in Latin **but** you are not in my class.

Forgive us our debts **as** we forgive our debtors.

Note: The words *etiam* and *non* are adverbs.

Vocabulary

1. sicut	as
2. et	and
3. sed	but
4. etiam	also
5. non	not

Latin Prayers (The Our Father or Lord's Prayer)

Panem nostrum cotidianum da nobis hodie

– Give us this day our daily bread.

Review Questions

1. What kind of word shows a relationship? _____

2. In what letter do all simple verbs end? _____

3. In what letter do nouns in our first group end? _____

4. What is the most important verb in any language? _____

5. What tense describes something that will happen? _____

Lesson 21 Exercises

Write a sentence in English with each of the vocabulary words in Lesson 21.

1. _____

2. _____

3. _____

4. _____

5. _____

Translate

1. sed _____

2. sicut _____

3. non _____

4. etiam _____

5. et _____

Speaking Latin --Listen to the Lesson 21 track on your Prima Latina CD--

- ☐ Say each vocabulary word and its meaning three times.
- ☐ Look for "E pluribus unum" on the dollar bill.

  Say this Latin phrase each time you buy something.

Write and Learn

1. Write each vocabulary word and its meaning twice.

   1. _____   _____

        _____   _____

   2. _____   _____

        _____   _____

   3. _____   _____

        _____   _____

   4. _____   _____

        _____   _____

   5. _____   _____

        _____   _____

Fun Practice

Fill in the blanks.

1. I am as _____ strong _____, as _____ .

2. I am good at _____ , and also _____ .

3. I like _____ , but I don't like _____ .

4. I am not _____ .

5. I also like _____ .

Practical Latin

Ego amo te   – I love you.

Lesson - Question Words

We ask questions when we want to find out information - when we want an answer.
The vocabulary for this lesson lists words that indicate a question in Latin.

We can recognize *question sentences* because they always have a **question mark.**
A **question mark** looks like this:

Examples:

Where are you going**?**

What school do you attend**?**

Why do you learn Latin**?**

Who is your teacher**?**

Vocabulary

1. quis	who?
2. quid	what?
3. ubi	where?
4. cur	why?

Latin Prayers (The Our Father or Lord's Prayer)

Et dimitte nobis debita nostra   – and forgive us our debts

Derivatives

inquisitive	-- questioning (adj.)
ubiquitous	-- seemingly everywhere (adj.)
query	-- question (n.)
curious	-- eager to know (adj.)

Review Questions

1. Practice counting 1-10 out loud in Latin.

2. Write the numbers 1-10 in Latin.

   1. _____   6. _____

   2. _____   7. _____

   3. _____   8. _____

   4. _____   9. _____

   5. _____   10. _____

3. What is the name for a group of stars that form a picture? _____

4. What is an English word that has a sound and meaning similar to a Latin word?

   _____

5. How do you say, "One out of many" in Latin? _____

Lesson 22 Questions

1. Why do you ask questions? _____

2. How can you tell if a sentence is a question? _____

3. How do you say, " I love you." in Latin? _____

Translate

1. ubi   _____

2. cur   _____

3. quis   _____

4. quid   _____

Speaking Latin --Listen to the Lesson 22 track on your Prima Latina CD--

☐ Say each vocabulary word and its meaning five times. Practice your pronunciation.

☐ This week, say, "I love you" in Latin to the people you care about.

Write and Learn

Write each vocabulary word and its meaning twice.

1. _____   _____
   _____   _____

2. _____   _____
   _____   _____

3. _____   _____
   _____   _____

4. _____   _____
   _____   _____

Fun Practice

Write down five questions you have. Make sure you use a *question mark* at the end of the sentence. Ask the questions to someone close to you to receive the information you want.

1. _____
2. _____
3. _____
4. _____
5. _____

Practical Latin

Optime!   – Excellent!

Lesson – The First Declension

In life, we use groups to help us keep information straight.

There are food groups (meats, dairy, grains, etc).

There are animal groups (birds, mammals, fish, etc).

There are even people groups (nations, cities, familes, friends).

There are also groups to help us keep Latin grammar straight.

> Verb groups are called **Conjugations.**
> Noun groups are called **Declensions.**

A **Declension** is a group of nouns that has the same or similar endings when declined. The most important thing to learn for now is that **declensions** go with **nouns** - people, places, or things.

There are only five declensions (or noun groups) in Latin.
On the next page the endings in the **First Declension Singular** are listed.
(Remember that singular means one, and the singular pronouns are I, you, he, she, it.)

By simply learning this list, you have made a big leap in Latin. We will explain declensions more next year as you progress in your Latin study.

Grammar

First Declension, Singular

a

ae

ae

am

a

(ae has the long **A** sound)

Latin Prayers (The Our Father or Lord's Prayer)

Sicut et nos dimittimus debitoribus nostris
 – As we also forgive our debtors.

Review Questions

1. Practice saying the first half of The Lord's Prayer from Lessons 16-20 plus what you have learned from Lessons 21-23. Write what you have learned from Lesson 21-23 once and translate it to English.

_____

_____

_____

_____

_____

_____

Lesson 23 Questions

1. What is the name for a group of nouns with the same endings?_____

2. What kind of word does a declension go with? _____

3. How many singular first declension endings are there? _____

Speaking Latin --Listen to the Lesson 23 track on your *Prima Latina* CD--

☐ Say the first declension singular endings five times. Practice your pronunciation.

☐ When you do something well this week, say, "Excellent!" in Latin.

Write and Learn

Write the first declension singular endings three times.

a	_____	_____	_____
ae	_____	_____	_____
ae	_____	_____	_____
am	_____	_____	_____
a	_____	_____	_____

Fun Practice

Think of a poem or song to help you remember the first declension singular endings.

Practical Latin

Pessime! — Very bad

Lesson – Declensions

Below is a list of the **First Declension Plural** endings.

(Remember *Plural* means more than one.)

Again, practice these from memory and watch your pronunciations.

Grammar

(Remember, **I** sounds like a long **E** in Latin.)

First Declension Plural Endings

ae

arum

is

as

is

You have now learned the endings for the entire First Declension. Congratulations!

Latin Prayers (The Our Father or Lord's Prayer)

Et ne nos inducas in tentationem — And lead us not into temptation

Review Questions

1. What does an **E** sound like in Latin? _____

2. What does an **I** sound like in Latin? _____

3. How do you say, "Repeat" in Latin? _____

4. How do you say, "Goodbye, friends" in Latin? _____

5. How many vowels are in the Latin alphabet? _____

Lesson 24 Questions

1. What does "plural" mean? _____

2. What kind of word goes with declensions? _____

3. How many first declension plural endings are there? _____

Speaking Latin --Listen to the Lesson 24 track on your Prima Latina CD-- _____

☐ Say the first declension plural endings five times. Practice your pronunciation.

☐ When you mess up this week say, "Pessime!"

Write and Learn

Write the first declension plural endings five times.

1. _____

2. _____

3. _____

4. _____

5. _____

Fun Practice

Add a line or verse to your poem or song from Lesson 23 to help you remember the first declension plural endings.

Practical Latin ⎯⎯⎯⎯⎯⎯⎯⎯⎯⎯⎯⎯⎯⎯⎯⎯⎯⎯⎯⎯

Finis!   – The End!

Lesson - First Conjugation ⎯⎯⎯⎯⎯⎯⎯⎯⎯⎯⎯⎯⎯⎯

As you know, conjugations are verb groups.

Conjugating means changing a verb based on *who* or *what* is doing the action and *when* that action actually occurs.

Example: Think of the word *walk*.

If you are talking about yourself, you say: "I *walk*."

If you are talking about your friend John, you say: "John *walks*."

See how you change (or **conjugate**) the verb because of *who* is doing the verb.

Let's do another one. The verb is *run*.

If your dog, Spot, runs, you say: "Spot *runs*."

If you run, you say: "I *run*."

If you run with your dog, you say: "We *run*."

A verb is also changed (or **conjugated**) because of *when* the verb happens. Look at the example below.

The verb is *call*.

If you called yesterday, you would say: "Yesterday I *called*."

If you are going to call tomorrow, you say: "Tomorrow I *will call*."

If you are calling right now, you say: "I *call*."

For now, the most important thing to remember is that **conjugations** go with **verbs**. We will talk more about **conjugations** as we learn more about the Latin language.

Grammar

These first conjugation verb endings are the pronoun letters from Lesson 13.

1. am**o**		I love
2. ama**s**		you love
3. ama**t**		he, she, it loves
4. ama**mus**		we love
5. ama**tis**		you (pl.) love
6. ama**nt**		they love

Latin Prayers (The Our Father or Lord's Prayer)

Sed libera nos a malo. Amen.   – But deliver us from evil. Amen.

Review Questions

1. What is an action word called? _____

2. What kind of word modifies a verb?_____

3. What kind of word modifies a noun or pronoun? _____

4. What comes at the end of all question sentences? _____

5. What kind of word does "declension" go with? _____

Lesson 25 Questions

1. What kind of word does "conjugation" go with? _____

2. What are two things that cause a verb to change or be conjugated?_____

_____

Translate

1. amas _____

2. amo _____

3. amamus _____

4. amatis _____

5. amant _____

6. amat _____

Speaking Latin --Listen to the Lesson 25 track on your Prima Latina CD--

☐ Say the first conjugation of "I love" five times. Practice your pronunciation.

☐ When you finish something this week, say, "Finis!"

Write and Learn

Write the first conjugation of "I love" three times in Latin.

_____   _____   _____

_____   _____   _____

_____   _____   _____

_____   _____   _____

_____   _____   _____

_____   _____   _____

Fun Practice

Draw a picture of a train with six cars. Put one form of "I love" in Latin in each car.

Be sure to put them in the order they are presented on the previous page.

Decorate your train any way you like.

Make a great caboose because you just ended your first year of Latin!

Vocabulary

Other Words

sicut	as
et	and
sed	but
etiam	also
non	not

Question Words

quis	who?
quid	what?
ubi	where?
cur	why?

First Declension Singular

a
ae
ae
am
a

First Declension Plural

ae
arum
is
as
is

First Conjugation

amo	I love
amas	you love
amat	he, she, it loves
amamus	we love
amatis	you (pl.) love
amant	they love

Latin Song-- More of the Refrain of "Resonet in Laudibus"
 Christus natus hodie--
 Christ is born today

Practical Latin

E pluribus unum	One out of many
Ego amo te.	I love you.
Optime!	Excellent!
Pessime!	Very bad!
Finis	The end!

Sayings and Prayers (The Lord's Prayer or Our Father)

Panem nostrum cotidianum da nobis hodie,	Give us this day our daily bread,
et dimitte nobis debita nostra	and forgive us our debts
sicut et nos dimittimus debitoribus nostris.	as we also forgive our debtors.
Et ne nos inducas in tentationem,	And lead us not into temptation,
sed libera nos a malo. Amen.	but deliver us from evil. Amen.

A. Copy all vocabulary words and translate.

Extra: Write one derivative next to each word.

	Word	Derivative	Translation
1.	_____	_____	_____
2.	_____	_____	_____
3.	_____	_____	_____
4.	_____	_____	_____
5.	_____	_____	_____
6.	_____	_____	_____
7.	_____	_____	_____
8.	_____	_____	_____
9.	_____	_____	_____

B. Answer the following questions.

1. What kind of word does **declension** go with? _____

2. What kind of word does **conjugation** go with? _____

3. What goes at the end of all question sentences? _____

4. What are two reasons why you would conjugate a verb in a sentence?_____

_____

C. Review the entire Lord's Prayer below. ***When you are ready,*** cover the prayer, write it once completely, and translate into English.

Pater Noster, qui es in caelis,	Our Father, who is in heaven,
sanctificetur nomen Tuum.	hallowed be Your name.
Adveniat regnum Tuum.	Your kingdom come.
Fiat voluntas Tua,	Your will be done,
sicut in Caelo et in terra.	on earth as it is in heaven.
Panem nostrum cotidianum da nobis hodie,	Give us this day our daily bread,
et dimitte nobis debita nostra	and forgive us our debts
sicut et nos dimittimus debitoribus nostris.	as we also forgive our debtors.
Et ne nos inducas in tentationem,	And lead us not into temptation,
sed libera nos a malo. Amen.	but deliver us from evil. Amen.

_____

_____

_____

_____

_____

_____

_____

_____

_____

_____

_____

_____

_____

D. Translate into Latin.

1. One out of many _____

2. I love you. _____

3. Excellent! _____

4. Very bad! _____

5. The end! _____

E. Lingua Angelica Extra:

Sing more of the Refrain of "Resonet in Laudibus."
Write the Latin words once and translate.

_____

_____

_____

_____

_____

_____

Notes

Appendix

VOCABULARY APPENDIX - ALPHABETICAL

adoro	*I adore*	verb (4)	**narro**	*I tell*	verb (5)
altus	*high, deep*	adjective (14)	**nauta**	*sailor*	noun (8)
ambulo	*I walk*	verb (1)	**navigo**	*I sail*	verb (3)
amo	*I love*	verb (4)	**non**	*not*	adverb (21)
aqua	*water*	noun (7)	**novem**	*nine*	adjective (10)
aquarius	*water carrier*	noun (16)	**novus**	*new*	adjective (14)
aries	*ram*	noun (16)	**numquam**	*never*	adverb (15)
bimus	*we will*	verb ending (20)	**nunc**	*now*	adverb (15)
bis	*you will*	vern ending (20)	**octo**	*eight*	adjective (10)
bit	*he, she, it will*	verb ending (20)	**oro**	*I pray*	verb (3)
bitis	*you will*	verb ending (20)	**paro**	*I prepare*	verb (4)
bo	*I will*	verb ending (20)	**patria**	*country*	noun (7)
bonus	*good*	adjective (14)	**pisces**	*fish*	noun (17)
bunt	*they will*	verb ending (20)	**porto**	*I carry*	verb (3)
caelum	*heaven*	noun (2)	**possum**	*I can*	verb (19)
cancer	*crab*	noun (16)	**possumus**	*we can*	verb (19)
capricorn	*goat*	noun (16)	**possunt**	*they can*	verb (19)
cena	*dinner*	noun (7)	**potes**	*you can*	verb (19)
clam	*secretly*	adverb (15)	**potest**	*he, she, it can*	verb (19)
clamo	*I shout*	verb (2)	**potestis**	*you can*	verb (19)
contra	*against*	preposition (12)	**pugno**	*I fight*	verb (5)
corona	*crown*	noun (7)	**quattuor**	*four*	adjective (9)
cur	*why*	adverb (22)	**quid**	*what*	adverb (22)
decem	*ten*	adjective (10)	**quinque**	*five*	adjective (9)
Deus	*God*	proper noun (1)	**quis**	*who*	pronoun (22)
duo	*two*	adjective (9)	**regina**	*queen*	noun (6)
es	*you are*	verb (18)	**Roma**	*Rome*	proper noun (11)
est	*he, she, it is*	verb (18)	**saepe**	*often*	adverb (15)
estis	*you are*	verb (18)	**sagittarius**	*archer*	noun (17)
et	*and*	conjunction (21)	**scorpio**	*scorpion*	noun (17)
etiam	*also*	adverb (21)	**sed**	*but*	conjunction (21)
ex	*out of*	preposition (12)	**semper**	*always*	adverb (15)
femina	*woman*	noun (8)	**septem**	*seven*	adjective (10)
fortuna	*luck*	noun (8)	**sex**	*six*	adjective (10)
geminus	*twin*	noun (16)	**sicut**	*as*	adverb (21)
gloria	*glory*	noun (2)	**silva**	*forest*	noun (6)
habito	*I live in*	verb (4)	**specto**	*I look at*	verb (3)
herba	*herb*	noun (8)	**stella**	*star*	noun (6)
Hispania	*Spain*	proper noun (11)	**sub**	*under*	preposition (12)
injuria	*injury*	noun (8)	**sum**	*I am*	verb (18)
inter	*between*	preposition (12)	**sumus**	*we are*	verb (18)
Italia	*Italy*	proper noun (11)	**sunt**	*they are*	verb (18)
Jesus	*Jesus*	proper noun (2)	**supero**	*I conquer*	verb (5)
judico	*I judge*	verb (4)	**supra**	*above*	preposition (12)
laboro	*I work*	verb (3)	**taurus**	*bull*	noun (17)
laudo	*I praise*	verb (2)	**terra**	*earth*	noun (6)
leo	*lion*	noun (17)	**toga**	*toga*	noun (1)
libero	*I free*	verb (5)	**tres**	*three*	adjective (9)
libra	*scales*	noun (17)	**ubi**	*where*	adverb (22)
longus	*long*	adjective (14)	**unda**	*wave*	noun (6)
luna	*moon*	noun (1)	**unus**	*one*	adjective (9)
Marcus	*Marcus*	proper noun (11)	**via**	*road*	noun (1)
Maria	*Mary*	proper noun (11)	**virgo**	*maiden, virgin*	noun (16)
mensa	*table*	noun (7)	**vita**	*life*	noun (6)
multus	*much, many*	adjective (14)	**voco**	*I call*	verb (5)

altus	*high, deep*	adjective (14)		**terra**	*earth*	noun (6)
bonus	*good*	adjective (14)		**toga**	*toga*	noun (1)
decem	*ten*	adjective (10)		**unda**	*wave*	noun (6)
duo	*two*	adjective (9)		**via**	*road*	noun (1)
longus	*long*	adjective (14)		**virgo**	*maiden, virgin*	noun (16)
multus	*much, many*	adjective (14)		**vita**	*life*	noun (6)
novem	*nine*	adjective (10)		**contra**	*against*	preposition (12)
novus	*new*	adjective (14)		**ex**	*out of*	preposition (12)
octo	*eight*	adjective (10)		**inter**	*between*	preposition (12)
quattuor	*four*	adjective (9)		**sub**	*under*	preposition (12)
quinque	*five*	adjective (9)		**supra**	*above*	preposition (12)
septem	*seven*	adjective (10)		**quis**	*who*	pronoun (22)
sex	*six*	adjective (10)		**Deus**	*God*	proper noun (1)
tres	*three*	adjective (9)		**Hispania**	*Spain*	proper noun (11)
unus	*one*	adjective (9)		**Italia**	*Italy*	proper noun (11)
clam	*secretly*	adverb (15)		**Jesus**	*Jesus*	proper noun (2)
cur	*why*	adverb (22)		**Marcus**	*Marcus*	proper noun (11)
etiam	*also*	adverb (21)		**Maria**	*Mary*	proper noun (11)
non	*not*	adverb (21)		**Roma**	*Rome*	proper noun (11)
numquam	*never*	adverb (15)		**adoro**	*I adore*	verb (4)
nunc	*now*	adverb (15)		**ambulo**	*I walk*	verb (1)
quid	*what*	adverb (22)		**amo**	*I love*	verb (4)
saepe	*often*	adverb (15)		**clamo**	*I shout*	verb (2)
semper	*always*	adverb (15)		**es**	*you are*	verb (18)
sicut	*as*	adverb (21)		**est**	*he, she, it is*	verb (18)
ubi	*where*	adverb (22)		**estis**	*you are*	verb (18)
et	*and*	conjunction (21)		**habito**	*I live in*	verb (4)
sed	*but*	conjunction (21)		**judico**	*I judge*	verb (4)
aqua	*water*	noun (7)		**laboro**	*I work*	verb (3)
aquarius	*water carrier*	noun (16)		**laudo**	*I praise*	verb (2)
aries	*ram*	noun (16)		**libero**	*I free*	verb (5)
caelum	*heaven*	noun (2)		**narro**	*I tell*	verb (5)
cancer	*crab*	noun (16)		**navigo**	*I sail*	verb (3)
capricorn	*goat*	noun (16)		**oro**	*I pray*	verb (3)
cena	*dinner*	noun (7)		**paro**	*I prepare*	verb (4)
corona	*crown*	noun (7)		**porto**	*I carry*	verb (3)
femina	*woman*	noun (8)		**possum**	*I can*	verb (19)
fortuna	*luck*	noun (8)		**possumus**	*we can*	verb (19)
geminus	*twin*	noun (16)		**possunt**	*they can*	verb (19)
gloria	*glory*	noun (2)		**potes**	*you can*	verb (19)
herba	*herb*	noun (8)		**potest**	*he, she, it can*	verb (19)
injuria	*injury*	noun (8)		**potestis**	*you can*	verb (19)
leo	*lion*	noun (17)		**pugno**	*I fight*	verb (5)
libra	*scales*	noun (17)		**specto**	*I look at*	verb (3)
luna	*moon*	noun (1)		**sum**	*I am*	verb (18)
mensa	*table*	noun (7)		**sumus**	*we are*	verb (18)
nauta	*sailor*	noun (8)		**sunt**	*they are*	verb (18)
patria	*country*	noun (7)		**supero**	*I conquer*	verb (5)
pisces	*fish*	noun (17)		**voco**	*I call*	verb (5)
regina	*queen*	noun (6)		**bimus**	*we will*	verb e
sagittarius	*archer*	noun (17)		**bit**	*he, she, it will*	verb
scorpio	*scorpion*	noun (17)		**bitis**	*you will*	ver
silva	*forest*	noun (6)		**bo**	*I will*	ve
stella	*star*	noun (6)		**bunt**	*they will*	
taurus	*bull*	noun (17)		**bis**	*you will*	

PRACTICAL LATIN SAYINGS- APPENDIX

Lesson	Practical Latin	Translation
1	Salve!	– Hello! (to one person)
	Salvete!	– Hello! (to more than one person)
2	Magister	– Teacher (male)
	Magistra	– Teacher (female)
3	Surge	– Stand up (one person)
	Surgite	– Stand up (more than one person)
4	Vale	– Goodbye (to one person)
	Valete	– Goodbye (to more than one person)
5	Discipulus	– student
	Discipuli	– students
	(sc has a 'sh' sound)	
6	Deo Gratias	– Thanks be to God
7	Mea Culpa	– my fault
8	amicus	– friend
	amici	– friends
9	Sedete	– Sit Down (to many)
10	Anno Domini, A.D.	– In the Year of our Lord
11	Veni, vidi, vici	– I came, I saw, I conquered. (Julius Caesar)
12	Quo vadis?	– Where are you going?
13	alma mater	– nurturing mother
14	Stupor Mundi	– wonder of the world
15	Nunc aut numquam	– Now or never
16	Semper Fidelis	– Always Faithful (Marine Corps motto)
17	Repetite	– Repeat (to many)
	Quid agis?	– How are you?
	Satis bene	– very well
	Romanus civis sum	– I am a citizen of Rome
	...ribus unum	– One out of many
	...o te	– I love you.
		– Excellent!
		– Very bad
		– The End!